Through the Tunnel

BECOMING DEAFBLIND

Angie C. Orlando

Handtype Press
Minneapolis, MN

Acknowledgments

The pieces "Doubt" and "Instrument of Choice" first appeared in *Wordgathering*.

I would like to thank Dr. Katherine Orr, my first writing teacher from Kent State University who opened my heart to the joys of writing; and to Jeanne Bryner, a local poet who enriched my craft through her books and passionate support.

I also wish to thank my friend, Leah Subak, who believed in me no matter what.

Copyright

Handtype Press
PO Box 3941
Minneapolis, MN 55403-0941
online: www.handtype.com
email: handtype@gmail.com

Printed in the United States of America
ISBN: 978-1-941960-11-0
Library of Congress Control Number: 2018949821

A Handtype Press First Edition

This book is dedicated to my brother,
Tony Orlando,
who died of suicide one week before his 39th birthday.

CONTENTS

Part One

Part Two

Part Three

Part One

In the Dark

Do you live in the dark? You expect me to say "Yes."

What does a blind person see? You think I'll say "Black."

I see swirls of psychedelic colors: hundreds of white Life Savers on a yellow background, with hues of pink and green peeking through the holes, red and blue spill across the scene, while purple and orange shoot from the bottom like flames, always moving, rolling, swirling ... So it goes on, and you might suspect I'm on a bad acid trip. Black would be a blessing.

Do you live in the dark? The answer is so simple, it sounds like a bad joke. I don't live in the dark. I always turn on a light.

If I wake up at 4:00 in the morning and need to use the bathroom, I switch on the bathroom light. I don't want to pee in the dark. Why is that so hard to understand?

Today, I'm coming in from the garage with extra toilet paper. As I stumble through the kitchen, I bump into a chair and fall. The four rolls of toilet paper go flying ... Don't ask me where, I'm blind, remember?

I'm on my hands and knees, feeling around for toilet paper. I bang my head repeatedly, because that's what happens when you crawl as a blind person. Rolls one and two turn up quickly. Roll three is tricky. God only knows where roll four landed. I continue to search on my knees with my hands outstretched, hitting my head and cursing.

During my frantic search, I invoke the name of God. Here I am on my hands and knees. Jehovah came forth and said "Rise, my daughter."

I didn't listen, because I'm deaf. No, actually, I'm blind. His witness says the end is coming soon. I must let Jehovah into my heart.

I say I'm doing fine without Him. Is that another cosmic joke? I'm blind, deaf and fallen. But I'm doing just fine, thank you for asking.

Do not fear, I am not in the dark. I turned on the kitchen light.

Disability Jam

Let's say there are two blind men in my living room. Finally, the repairmen are here to fix the blinds my cat destroyed. Blinds are found on windows. Two men who are blind refer to people.

If there are two people who are blind in the living room, how many cats are in the room? Zero—both men have guide dogs.

Now there's a deaf girl in the kitchen. She ignores you. Say there is a girl who is deaf in the kitchen. She glares at you. She's a grown woman. If there is a woman who is deaf in the kitchen, how many people are there? Two—she has a sign language interpreter.

Now we are in a meeting with seven people and three wheelchairs. How many people are in the room? Ten —there are people sitting in those wheelchairs.

Say there are three wheelchair-bound people in a room. Call 911! It's illegal to bind people to wheelchairs.

Now we see a person who is blind, a woman who is deaf, a man in a wheelchair and a teen with autism. How many service dogs are in the room? Four— the person who is blind has a Seeing Eye Dog. The woman who is deaf has a Hearing Dog. The man in a wheelchair uses a Mobility Assistance Dog. The teen with autism has an Autism Assistance Dog.

Let's say there is a Muslim woman who is blind. How many guide dogs are in the room? Zero—Islamic law prohibits Muslims from owning dogs. This woman uses a specially trained miniature pony.

5

Say there is a man in a wheelchair who is quadriplegic. What kind of dog does he have? None—he uses a Helping Hands Monkey Helper.

So there are five people in the room, and you say they all look normal. How many have disabilities? Five—one has low vision. Another is hard of hearing. The third has a learning disability. The next person has a mental illness. The last one has a health impairment.

What if there are 100 people in an auditorium and none have disabilities. How many are normal? None.

The Slide
Longcoy Elementary School, 1983

Curly, brown-haired Megan is eight, a year younger than me. Her sister Mary is six and still sucks her thumb. They go everywhere without shoes, the soles of their feet black from dirt and grime. I have no sympathy when they complain about hot pavement or a sharp stone. "Put on some stupid shoes" I say.

The dodge ball court is filled with wood planks and gym equipment tied under blue tarps. A sign reads "Do not climb on the equipment." We climb on the equipment.

I'm struggling to open a crate, looking for a tetherball set. Mary swings one-handed around a tall pole, her other hand pressed to face as she sucks her thumb. Megan cups her eyes, gazing up the hill into my backyard where my brothers play whiffle ball. Tony swings the bat and misses, Scott pumps his arm in triumph.

Mary asks "Is Steve over there?"

I peer around the wall at the corner of the school. "He's not there" I tell her.

I don't know who Steve is or where he came from. He appeared at the school one day, sitting in his wheelchair at the corner, an adult with unkempt hair and drool on his chin, watching kids play.

"He's scary" Mary says around her thumb.

"He's crazy and retarded" Megan declares. "Papa says he escaped from an institution."

The sky begins to darken, we are the only kids at the school. Suddenly, Steve rolls onto the black top, racing across the playground in a new electric wheelchair. We scream, girl shrieks of laughter and fear. Steve ignores us, disappears around the building.

Ten minutes later, he makes another pass across the playground, singing in a thick, slurred voice "These days are ours happy and free oh happy days ..." Steve rolls out of sight.

"What an idiot" Megan scoffs.

I say "The big dummy likes his new wheels."

Mary whines "I wanna go home he scares me."

Steve has lapped the school again, starts past the playground, still singing his song.

I bellow, garbled and off-key "Sunday Monday happy days ..."

Megan yells "Idiot retard go away dummy!" She chases him around swings and a slide.

We hear a wordless, terrifying scream of rage. I stop singing, mouth agape. Steve whips around in his wheelchair, swiftly moving over the bumpy concrete. Megan leaps onto the small, yellow slide, climbs safely to the top. He turns toward the dodge ball court, coming at us, top speed.

Mary freezes, both hands grip the pole, knuckles turn white. I pry her fingers apart, pull her away. We run, Steve right behind.

Megan screams "Help help!" I reach the bottom of

the slide, jump on. Mary has one leg up when Steve runs over her other foot.

I wrench her arm, and she lands on the slide, screaming, she clings to my legs two feet from the edge. Blood trickles down the dented, silver surface.

Steve hits the lower side of the slide again and again. Megan continues to yell "Help help help!"

Mary shrieks "Mommy! Mommy!"

Steve roars. I both hear and feel the thud thud thud of the wheelchair hitting the slide.

Tony and Scott charge across the pavement, wielding plastic baseball bats. Steve zooms away around the corner, Tony chasing after him. Scott scoops up Mary, sprints toward her house. Megan climbs down the ladder, I push myself over the side, not wanting to get blood on my clothes.

Neighbors rush to the playground. People ask "Are you okay? What happened? Did he hurt you?"

A man growls "I'm going to kill that fucking retard."

Tears sting my eyes, legs feel like rubber. I collapse to the pavement, touch the deep dent Steve made in the peeling yellow-painted slide.

Family History

Doctor: To begin this case study, tell me when the pathogen first became apparent.

Student: In the oldest brother, age 12, Retinitis Pigmentosa.

Doctor: And what is that? What are the symptoms?

Student: Known as RP, symptoms include gradual loss of peripheral vision and night blindness.

Doctor: His hearing?

Student: Better than average. Other brother is not affected.

Doctor: What of the patient?

Student: Daughter, youngest child, hearing loss age 13, diagnosed with RP at 16.

Doctor: How did this progress?

Student: Slowly, she could still read print in late 20s, understood speech with cochlear implant.

Doctor: Then what happened?

Student: Like her body shut down, total deafness, blindness, neuropathy in legs, feet, hands.

Doctor: Can she walk?

Student: Not on her own. Wears orthopedics, uses a forearm crutch, needs a sighted guide.

Doctor: Possible reasons for the sudden flare-up?

Student: Child birth six months prior, high levels of stress.

Doctor: What is the diagnosis?

Student: Unknown for a long time, frequently misdiagnosed. Blood tests positive for rare genetic mutation.

Doctor: What mutation?

Student: Name is PHARC, hearing loss, RP, neuropathy, it all fits.

Doctor: Does the brother test positive?

Student: We don't know, he's deceased of unrelated causes.

Doctor: Let's examine our patient.

Summer Vacation with Katie's Family

We squish into the back seat of Mr. Rowe's small car. Me and Katie are mighty cool, 'cause we'll be starting junior high soon. Erin and Polly are going into eighth grade. They tell us stories about school, like we have to buy elevator tickets from the older kids. I'm not stupid, my brothers went to Davey, so I know the school doesn't have elevators.

"If you get caught in the bathroom with an eighth grader, she can give you a swirly" says Erin.

Polly touches my head, says "You can't be a cheerleader with short hair."

I duck and make puking sounds. "Cheerleading sucks I'm gonna join the soccer team."

Erin and Polly start clapping their hands, stomping their feet and chant "We've got spirit, S P I R I T spirit!"

Mr. Rowe yells "Knock it off" from the front seat.

We drive two hours through forest and Amish country to reach the camp. Katie's cousin came with Mrs. Rowe in a camper. He's eight, lives in Dayton, I call him Devon Dayton. He likes to fish, climb trees, and jump in mud puddles, same as me.

Mr. and Mrs. Rowe sleep in the camper, the rest of us share a big tent. Devon has to close his eyes when we dress. Katie screams "Naked girls" and he dives head first into his sleeping bag.

I've been growing and don't have many clothes.

Every day I wear my purple jams with palm trees and surfers, and a yellow shirt showing a shark in a canoe. I don't like the dark pink t-shirt that goes with the dark pink shorts, 'cause I got clay on it at Girl Scout day camp, and now it's kinda orange. Someone teased me about my turquoise shorts, so I won't wear them anymore.

Mom bought bras, I stuffed them in the back of my closet. Why'd she have to buy them? I only have a tiny bit of flesh betraying my girlhood. If I wear a bra, boys will make fun of my "over the shoulder pebble holder."

At camp, we make an Indian shelter in the woods. It looks so real, someone will find it later and call the newspaper about this ancient Indian settlement.

We use sticks, stuff leaves in the cracks, add rocks at the base because it keeps falling down.

Erin goes searching for branches and finds a rubber floating in a puddle. Devon is too young, but the rest of us go have a look. I know it's sex but can't figure out how, and I thought rubbers were blue.

Katie is scared the guy will come back for it. Erin says "That's dumb, guys only use a rubber once." She hooks the flaccid thing on the end of a stick, takes it to a trash can.

In the evening, Katie scolds me, 'cause I won't weave placemats out of long plants for our Indian house. I say "I'm a warrior not a weaver." Devon runs around the campfire making Indian sounds. He's got chocolate smeared all over his face from eating five s'mores.

Erin says "Don't touch the mats you'll get marshmallow on them, and Indians didn't eat marshmallows."

After a few days, I start to stink, I don't know why, but it smells awful. Katie pulls me away, says "You have BO."

I tell her "I do not, I've never had BO."

She says "It's your shirt, you need clean clothes."

I take a shower, put on my dark pink shorts and dark pink shirt, even though it looks kinda orange. Polly says "You look pretty."

Erin says "You should wear pink more often."

Devon says "You don't smell no more." Erin slaps her hand over his mouth.

We go to the rec center for the weekly movie. *Back to the Future*, I've seen it six times already, but that's okay. The movie starts, "Power of Love" blasts through the room. Katie says "Michael J. Fox is gorgeous."

I say "Who cares about that, look at him skateboard. Do you think I can do that when we get home?"

Photograph for Grandma
Grandma's house, 1986

Two boys stand on sunny patio
Younger sister sits in white wicker chair

The oldest brother, age 17,
Eyes fixed to the side
Peering through the distance, 100 miles
Longing for the girlfriend
He can't live without
Hair dark
Brown-rimmed glasses
Wearing navy-striped polo shirt
With a grimace on his face
Parents say two days away won't hurt
Since his first sweet taste of sex
Two minutes become too much

His brother, at 16,
Knows how to play
Angry over missing soccer game
Still willing to model for Grandma
Black hair styled carefully
Enhancing his Italian looks
Wearing a blue t-shirt
White jacket sleeves rolled up
Don Johnson in Steubenville Vice
Refuses to smile
Purses his lips
A calculated pose of coolness

The girl, age 12,
Face aglow
Innocent childish smile
Basking in Grandma's glory
Wearing royal blue sweat suit

Showcasing the blue in her eyes
Black hair ringlets of curls
Clutching in her arms
Favorite Cabbage Patch doll
Its bonnet off
Revealing yellow tufts of yarn hair

Voice Mail

Good morning, this is Kathy from the PHARC Clinic reminding you of your appointment on Wednesday at 10:30 AM. Please arrive 15 minutes early and bring your polyneuropathy, hearing loss, ataxia, retinitis pigmentosa and cataracts. Thanks so much, have a wonderful day.

How I Became A Girl

Before school starts, Mom takes me shopping for clothes. Instead of going to the girls' section at O'Neils we go to Gold Circle, and she let's me shop in the juniors department. I buy designer jeans, a one piece yellow shirt and white vest and another, looks like red t-shirt under red and white sweatshirt.

I fall in love with a white sweater, rainbow stripes and purple button down shirt to match. Mom breaks down, let's me get purple socks and purple earrings.

Late at night, I put on my new clothes, admiring myself in the full length mirror. Decision time, what is the perfect outfit for the first day of junior high?

Mom says I can't wear the white and rainbow sweater. "It's August you'll die from heat." I wear it anyway. By 4th period, I'm ready to pass out.

In English, I notice a boy named Sam sitting behind me. He's short, has strawberry blonde hair. Right away, he catches my eye, says "I like your sweater."

"I like your freckles" I blurt out, bury my face in my arms, so he won't see me blushing.

At home, I stop hiding my deodorant. It's a hassle crawling under the bed to dig it out of the hole in my mattress. I wear a bra to school, take it off before I go home. Soon discover it's more comfortable, wear them all the time.

When I get my first period, it's brown and frothy. I don't know what's wrong, so I take a bath every night. Mom says a bath can cure anything. The second time, it's thick, red, and I understand. I don't tell anyone, just steal Mom's pads, and that works out okay.

My parents buy three reserved seating season passes to the high school football games. Scott plays bass drum in the band. Tony sits with the Roosevelt kids. I want to sit in the junior high section. Mom asks the stupidest thing, "Are you sure you're old enough to be alone?"

Shooting her a look, I say "I'll be with my friends."

Dad sings "The gang's all here at Davey Jr. High ..." I want to crawl under the stadium, never come out.

Sam and I always sit together. We yell and holler for the Rough Riders, high five when they get a touchdown. One night he takes my hand, and I'm floating. I don't know if Roosevelt won, I don't care.

In October, Sam makes an invitation in Art class asking me to the school dance. I write "Yes," draw hearts all over a piece of notebook paper.

Neither of us knows how to dance, we kind of shuffle our feet. Katie gestures for me to put my head on Sam's shoulder, but he's so short. Finally, I get my head low enough. He smells like sweat and Prell shampoo. Maybe being a girl isn't so bad after all.

Instrument of Choice

I'm thin and scrawny, always looking up, searching the line of trumpets for cute boys, too shy to say hi, but I wave to the fat boy, my friend, who plays clarinet.

I wanted a voice, so I chose the huge sax, baritone, big as me. Neck aches from the weight, ankle twists with the strain to stay upright, fingers spread over keys the size of silver dollars, mouth bulges, tongue strokes reed. It tastes like wood, feels just right.

I gather breath from way down low, let it out with a soul-filled blow. Notes explode, strong and deep. I'm the beat, they follow my lead, flutes trill, trumpets buzz the melody.

I wanted a voice, so I chose the huge sax, and Ms. Hazel, the English teacher, says she can hear me from her room on the second floor.

—after Robert Phillips

Best Friends

Chioma lives two houses down on Gardenview Drive, a street with no gardens, nothing to view. She is the youngest and only girl in her family. Chioma has three brothers, I can't tell the twins apart. I've got two brothers, she can't tell them apart even though they aren't twins.

I want to be Chioma's twin. "Never say things like that" Mom warns me.

We go swimming at the high school pool. My swim suit is red and white striped, Chioma's is green. "Last one in is a rotten fish egg" I call, as I jump into the pool. Her cannonball dive sends water splashing everywhere.

At second break, we buy square pizzas with little bits of pepperoni. I say "That boy is staring at you."

"No he isn't."

"Yes he is."

She looks sick, tosses her pizza on my lap when he sits on the bench beside her, a pack of Reese's Peanut Butter Cups in his hand. Stanley is athletic, well-built, and I can tell Chioma likes him. His cousin is fat and can't swim.

When we go back in the pool, Stanley tosses Chioma around in the water. I think she's blushing, but it's hard to tell. Herman throws me too hard, and I get bruises on my arms. I want to escape to the deep end. "Stay with me" Chioma begs.

Chioma babbles about Stanley the whole way home. She's holding the Reese's cups he gave her. I offer to buy it, she refuses. "You're allergic to peanuts, what are you going to do with it?" I demand.

"I just want to keep it" she says with a goofy look on her face.

I'm home ten minutes when Chioma calls. "Stanley wants to see *Some Kind of Wonderful* with me, you have to come." Mom says I can, so we make plans to meet the boys tomorrow afternoon.

Later, Mom comes into my room, sits on the bed. "Honey, are these boys black?"

I'm caught off guard. What kind of questions is that? "Yeah" I say.

"I was afraid of that. You are not going to the movie."

I jump up, my head spinning with anger and confusion. "Why can't I go?"

"It wouldn't look right for a white girl to be with black boys."

I don't know what to say. Chioma is black, and I hang out with her all the time.

Mom stands and walks to the door, turning back to look at me. "White boys don't like girls who run around with black boys. Stay away from those kids."

On the Bus

The old Kent City school bus shakes and rattles down pockmarked Ada Drive. Rowdy junior high students shout, pound fists against green seats.

"Call me" a girl yells to someone as she gets off.

"Damn it! I forgot my math book" bellows a boy in the back, while his friends jeer at him.

Eric, jean jacket collar up, Walkman head phones snug over his ears, sings "You gotta fight for your right to party."

I sit in the middle, my body slightly touching the brown haired boy beside me. Chioma, arms crossed over chest, stares at us from across the aisle, and I look down. The line of silver duct tape covering a tear in the seat becomes the most fascinating thing I've ever seen. I finger the frayed edges, bits of dirty stuffing popping out at the side.

"Go on" she urges "kiss her."

Mike mumbles "Do you want to?" He's so close I can smell the spicy scent of his deodorant.

"It's the next step, you have to do it" Chioma insists.

Mike leans in, lightly touching his lips against mine, soft and wet, like nothing I've ever felt before. The kiss is over in an instant.

Chioma cheers "Bravo!" She grabs my arm, pulls me backwards off the bus, my gaze still fixed on Mike's thin face and almond-shaped green eyes.

Part Two

Tinnitus

I struggle to sleep in the baking heat of another humid summer night. Both windows are open but offer no relief, not a single fresh breeze. I turn over again, wipe sweat off my brow and wish like crazy I had a fan.

The first helicopter flies overhead in June. It circles endlessly above the house, night after night. Soon there are more, two three five maybe ten. How can anyone sleep with those damn helicopter blades going round and round?

I look into my parents' room. Dad is asleep on his back, the yellow sheet rises and falls with each breath. Mom is on her side, one hand resting on the book she was reading when she fell asleep. The two big dogs lie quiet, one on the blue rug, the other half under the bed.

Our local newspaper says nothing about helicopters invading Ohio. By July, the racket grows louder. There must be dozens of them. I stick my head out the window, all I see are street lights and stars.

Desperate, I ask Chioma "What's with the helicopters at night?"

"What helicopters?" she asks. "All I hear is Mrs. Brown's bug zapper."

My heart is pounding. "Can't you hear the helicopters?"

"What are you talking about? Are you losing your mind girl?"

I force a smile, say "Psych! I almost got you."

That night, in my hot, dark room, I fear Chioma is right, I'm losing my mind, because the rhythmic sound of helicopters fills my head.

whop whop whop whop

Misdiagnosis Salad

1. Begin with a base of crisp Usher syndrome.

2. Add diced Guillain-Barré syndrome and sliced mitochondrial myopathy.

3. Mix in chunks of carpal tunnel syndrome.

4. Layer with shredded tendonitis. (For best results, use both tennis and golfer's elbow.)

5. Include bits of rotator cuff sprain and one cup chopped bursitis.

6. Stir in some vitamin D deficiency.

7. Cover with myalgia. (For a bolder taste, use fibromyalgia.)

8. Finally, sprinkle with insomnia and restless leg syndrome.

Recommendation: Share with your favorite quack. This salad is *de rigueur* when served with duck soufflé.

Voice Mail

Hello, this is Nurse Calloway from Neurology with your test results. As you may recall, Dr. Henry was concerned about degenerative brain damage. There was no evidence of this on your CT scan. However, the test revealed an anomaly: you have a cochlear implant. Please call us if you have any questions. Bye-bye.

Boys

1. Ryan

Ryan is a scrawny, little thing in other-sized clothes like an orphan from old TV shows. I watch him brush sandy brown hair away from his big, brown eyes. His shirt sleeves are too long, only the tips of his skeletal fingers are visible. I don't stop to wonder why he wears long sleeves in June.

Ryan gets mad when I ask why he's always missing school. Dad knows, but he won't tell. "Ryan and his mother have issues to work out" is all he says.

For the last day of 7th grade, Ryan begs me to wear my jeans with the suspenders and a red polo shirt. "You look great in that outfit. It's how I want to remember you."

"What do you mean? I'll be here next year, and we can get together during the summer." He doesn't say anything.

I want to make him happy, but everyone wears crazy clothes on the last day. I wear yellow jams and a blue t-shirt. Ryan is disappointed. I lie, tell him the suspenders broke.

He lies by not telling me he's about to move to California to live with an uncle. I learn about that from the only letter he sends me, right before the part about breaking up.

2. Charlie

Charlie isn't like my other boyfriends. He's tall, well-built and has wavy dark hair. I know he was held back a year in elementary school. He has gym 8th period, which means he's in a low-level reading class.

We hang out in the band room during lunch with a bunch of other kids. It's not as loud in there. Most of my old friends, like Jenna and Shelley, don't talk to me anymore, because I can't hear them in the cafeteria. They don't like me asking "What? What?" all the time. Charlie and the rest of the "band geeks" aren't as mean.

In 7th period band class, we march around the neighborhood to prepare for the Memorial Day parade. Charlie is hard to miss with a giant sousaphone wrapped around his body. I never thought I would like a tuba player.

He gets to leave ten minutes early for swimming class at the high school. He jumps in front of the saxophones, says something before dashing inside. I don't know what he said, but I'm sure he was talking to me. When we return to the band room, I find a folded piece of paper in my sax case. "Well, I guess I'm in love with you ..." I read 20 times.

Natalie says "Be careful, he was all over his last girlfriend."

"He wouldn't do that to me" I insist. I've only kissed one boy, that's as far as I want to go.

Charlie kisses me the next day. He's always got his hands on me, even in front of other people. Chioma says "Get a room!"

Charlie wants me to go to his house after school "My mom isn't home." I don't do it.

We've been together for a week, when he pulls me into the orchestra room after school, starts kissing me. The teacher comes in yelling "Get out you pigs!"

I want to get on the bus, but he isn't done. Charlie drags me into a dark band hallway, traps me in a corner with his body, kissing with passion. I squirm, try to get away, he's too strong.

He forces his tongue in my mouth, rubs my chest. My cries are lost in his greedy mouth. When a science teacher breaks it up, I run, jump on the bus as it's pulling away.

I don't want to go to school the next day, pretend to be sick, but Mom doesn't buy it. "You look fine except for your eyes, have you been crying?" I leave the house without answering. She probably thinks I didn't hear her.

All day, kids laugh and jeer. Natalie says "Charlie is bragging about how far he got with you."

Mr. Allen, the science teacher, keeps saying "Charlie Charlie Charlie" to get my attention. He doesn't understand what really happened.

When I get my 8th grade yearbook, I cover Charlie's picture with blue ink scribbles. I never want to see his face again.

3. David

I meet Darla first, she's in half my classes in 7th and 8th grade. She says "You're in the band, do you know my brother?"

I discover I do, David is a trumpet player who hangs out with Adam and Ryan. I talk to him all the time and didn't know he and Darla are twins.

I go swimming at her house the summer before starting high school. I want to flirt with David, but he never comes out of his room. He doesn't talk during dinner.

At band camp, I joke around with David, think maybe he likes me back, since he let me take his picture. It was windy, and his brown hair doesn't look as slicked back as usual. I pin the photo on my bulletin board.

I never thought about going to Homecoming. Natalie keeps bugging me to ask David. I say "No don't say anything to him!"

An older girl, David's squad leader, thinks I should go with him too. "He's cute and doesn't have a date," she says. I shake my head, too timid to speak to a senior.

When we get back from the band show late Saturday night, I walk alone toward the school doors. David comes over, puts his face right in front of mine. "NO!" he shouts and walked away.

4. Ryan Again

It's one week into the second semester of 9th grade. Nobody talks to me in the halls anymore. I barely notice all the faces that pass by, blending into each other.

I yelp when someone grabs my arm, David says "I called you three times." I don't want to talk to him, turn to leave, but there's a tall boy with short, sandy brown hair standing behind me. I don't know him. Why's he smiling like that?

Both boys laugh at my confusion. I think David is playing a trick on me but realize the boy is Ryan. "Wow you are tall" I say like an idiot. His lips move, I don't understand. "What did you say? What?"

Later, Ryan gives me a note. He's living in a foster home in Kent now. "I'm back ..."

It's just like 7th grade, but it's not. How do I explain? "My hearing went out my ear" I write back. God how lame!

We drop notes in each other's locker. "Can I call you tonight" he wants to know.

"No I'm not allowed to talk on the phone" I lie.

"Can you meet me at a movie on Sunday?" He draws a heart before his name.

Dad doesn't ask who I'm meeting, I don't tell. Adam is with Ryan, I don't mind, mostly glad it's not David. We share popcorn, hold hands. After the movie, the three of us take a walk along the Cuyahoga river. I keep tripping, so Ryan takes my hand, helps me over the uneven earth. The boys talk, while I concentrate on not falling.

I'm totally happy, can't wait to see Ryan on Monday.

Adam brings me a note in Biology, which is strange. My stomach churns with dread. The note says "Yesterday was horrible. I don't like being around you because you ignore everything I say. What was with the helpless girl act by the river? You aren't the person I used to love." He does not add a heart before his name.

Before the Lawn Chair Concert
Davey Jr. High School

Lazily, we take our places among yellow dandelions
on a field of grass before the audience arrives.

I'm dripping sweat in early June, evening sun. We
fiddle around, chatting, blowing lewd notes because
we are 14 and can.

The weight of this big sax hangs heavily on my neck,
long body bumping relentlessly against my leg.

Not a formal affair, we strip down to shorts and
t-shirts, ready to jazz it up as the sun goes down.

I glance behind me at Rob, heating up his trombone,
sliding it out, fully extended.

His soccer shorts flap wide at the thigh, white skin
disappears into a cavern of darkness.

Mr. Murphy calls us to attention. I lick my lips, deep
throat the massive mouthpiece and begin to blow.

Cochlear Implant, Age 16

Flat on my back
On a hospital gurney
Flying high
Zig-zagging through the sky

Surgeon, surgeon
I see you!

Yellow shower cap
Bug-eyed goggles
Flowing gown
Rubber gloves

You show off your pearly whites
Thousand dollar smile
I laugh and laugh
Far gone on the gas

Are you real?
Who can say?
I left my head
You will soon be dead

Time to work
Count back from ten
It's too late
I'm gone at eight

My hair shaved
Skin a flap
With tools in hand
You screwed around

Charge me a mint
Little plane you buy

In the air you flash
On the ground you crash

Teenage Girl as High School Scenery

I am the door you walk through each day. You open and close me, never notice the unique quality of my wood.

I am the blue carpet you walk upon, the plastic chair you sit in, the desk you use as a drawing board. I wear ink flowers, hearts, the name of your beloved.

I am the stiff, white chalk you break, smash into the rug, because you like the attention. You feel nothing while grinding me into the ground.

I am the gray waste basket where you throw away your droppings. Sometimes you kick me, because you know you can.

I am the Shakespeare poster on the wall, put there to cover a blemish long ago. You have yet to read my words.

I am the cobwebs on the ceiling, the dust on the blinds, the shadow in the corner. I grace your presence daily, never do you see me.

Marching Band

Long whistle blow
We snap to attention
Feet together
Head up
Go Kent!

My gloved hands eager
On pearly saxophone keys
Hot head under cowboy hat
Rough Rider coat with tails
Black pants, red stripe
Black shoes, white spats

Three short whistle blows
Lead snare drums cadence
As one, we lift instruments
Step onto field

Forward march 20!
Right pinwheel!
Left slant!
Mark time 24!

We play "Eye of the Tiger" and "Heart's on Fire"
Loud music fills the warm September night
My heart pulses with the thrill
Being part of something
Feels electrifying

Manic cheerleaders with big hair
Bounce onto field in tiny skirts
Hold painted paper tunnel

We blare out the notes
Roosevelt High School Victory song
Football players run
Break through tunnel
The crowd is pumped
Waving arms, screaming

  K.,
   K. E.,
    K. E. N. T.

300 legs fall still
Climax, drop to one knee
Back on feet, ready to move
Drummers hit the beat
The band marches on

Doubt

I doubt because of my sixth grade teacher, who asked "Did you proofread?" and I thought she was praising me, until she put my book report on the overhead projector. Red marker held in a wrinkled hand, she said "A student, someone sitting in this class, wrote this paper and did not proofread. Let's read together to find all the errors." My classmates turned around in their mismatched wooden desks, trying to spot the bad writer. I looked, too, holding back tears and hoped no one saw the shame on my face.

I doubt because of my report cards, how they were once filled with A's, when I was still whole. Then the B's and C's crept in, taken over by D's and F's as my hearing loss progressed, and how I'd have no paper to turn in, because I didn't know about the assignment, and the teacher confirmed my fault by giving me a zero.

I doubt because of my first love, the man who became my husband, who told me I was stupid and ugly, "Do you even have a brain? Are you retarded? How can you be so dumb?" The finger that poked me in the chest, the hands that pushed me down, the palm that slapped my face, and how he said "No one else will ever love you" and I believed him, because I was afraid not to.

I doubt because of the professor who told me to write only about overcoming my disabilities, how he said "People want to read about your hardships, not your life" and "This is what makes you different from other writers" and how he made me feel like a pair of damaged ears and broken eyes.

I doubt because of my writing mentor, who loved everything I wrote, and said "This is inspirational" and "You are so amazing." I begged for real feedback, but she said everything was perfect, until I wrote about the negative implications of being disabled, and how she said "You are disturbing, don't ever contact me again."

Faith

*So do not fear, for I am with you; do not be dismayed,
for I am your God. I will strengthen you and help you; I
will uphold you with my righteous right hand.*
—Isaiah 41:10

*Cast thy burden upon the LORD, and he shall sustain
thee: he shall never suffer the righteous to be moved.*
—Psalm 55:22

I

Summer of 2007, I sit in a lounge at a training center
for people who are deafblind. A man says "My name
is Michael. Are you Christian?"

There's that awkward moment of silence, my mind
races. What can I say? I go for what he wants to
hear.

"Yes, I'm Christian." We become good friends.

II

I was born into the Roman Catholic Church. I've seen
pictures of an adorable baby girl in a white dress.
The perfect handwriting on the back reads: Baptism,
1974.

There's another picture of me at my first Communion.
The girl wears a red plaid dress, white lace collar and
black ribbon. She has smooth, black hair, brown-
rimmed glasses and a shy smile.

Inside, she's screaming "Get me out of this church! Get me out of this dress!" The moment she reached home, she ripped off the dress, put on dirty jeans, a Charlie's Angels t-shirt and Cleveland Indians baseball cap.

III

We soon stopped going to church. My brothers had soccer games on Sundays. Mom needed to grocery shop, Dad had to mow the lawn before it rained.

I had to attend CCD on Wednesday nights. My parents believed everything was fine as long as I went to CCD and got Confirmed.

IV

There's no picture of my first, and only, confession. I don't know what I was wearing. I remember how nervous I was when I meekly confessed "My family doesn't go to church, not even on holidays."

There, I said it. Would God strike me down? The priest spoke softly "God is understanding, recite the Hail Mary ten times, and God will forgive you."

V

What is faith? I didn't learn the answer during CCD. Most of the time, we colored pictures of Jesus, rainbows and animals.

One teacher had long, stringy hair and bad body odor. He'd scream scripture at us. We didn't know what he was babbling about. We were ten and stared at the spittle in his beard.

One night after an hour of this, he said "The question is on the floor." We dropped to the floor, crawling around, looking for the question.

VI

When I was in 7th grade, there were no 8th graders, so 7th and 9th grade were placed in a class together. I was intimidated by the older students. I was just beginning junior high. They were starting high school. I was small with a little girl's body. They were tall and well-developed.

Our class was in the kitchen. The door was thick, opened with a loud squeal. No one could sneak up on us. We opened our books, and Doug, the teacher, led us on a discussion about sex or something equally inappropriate.

I remember one night, I was sitting there with a huge chunk of cotton between my legs, my first period. I didn't feel like a woman. I was miserable. The pad was uncomfortable. What if it leaked? Could people smell the blood?

Doug began telling period jokes. He knew ... I was sure of it. I wanted to disappear. Is that what it felt like to have faith?

VII

Doug was our teacher again the following year. They put us in the atrium right off the foyer, he had to behave. But being out in the open attracted the attention of Sister "mean" Jean. She knew I didn't go to church. Every Wednesday, she made me stand in front of the class, instructed me to summarize Sunday's sermon. I stood there, head down, shuffling my feet, silent, until she'd yell at me for being a sinner. I was fine with the sin. I just wanted out of the spotlight.

Hello? This was 8th grade. Didn't she know? Didn't everyone know what that meant? I felt like a neon sign flashed over my head: Losing her hearing.

It should have said "Losing her religion."

VIII

I refused to go to CCD. In 9th grade, Mom expected me to return two years later for Confirmation classes. By this point, I was deaf and losing my peripheral vision. God was not my friend. I had no intention of being Confirmed.

My mother pleaded "It's an important sacrament. Just get Confirmed, then you can leave the church."

This made no sense. Confirmation is about agreeing with the Catholic church and accepting God into your life. I couldn't go through that knowing it wasn't real. It would be hypocritical. To a teenager, that's the worst sin a person can commit.

IX

In high school, I was friends with a group of girls who were deeply religious. One day, we were passing around a notebook during chemistry, and the subject of religion came up. I asked "What is faith? How do you find faith?"

Another girl answered "How can you not have faith?"

I think my questions offended her. She didn't understand that I was sincere.

X

My husband and I were married in an Episcopal church in Chaptico, Maryland. Built in the 17th century, the church had a sense of history that was overwhelming. I liked Sean, the minister. Although I didn't take Communion, I allowed him to bless me. This, I believed, was the path to faith.

In late 2001, my precious son, Joseph, was christened in the same church. He, too, became a part of history.

I asked Sean to pray for me. Something was wrong, my vision and hearing loss rapidly getting worse. I had trouble walking, my body hurt. Only God could save me.

A few days later, I was hospitalized. After a week, they sent me home where I would be "more comfortable." Sean came to visit. I was desperate and scared. As he prayed over my feet, I asked "Why does God want me to suffer?"

Sean gently took my hand and said "God loves you."

I laughed hysterically. What kind of crap was that? If

God loved me, He would not make me hurt. He would not take away my hearing and vision. He would not leave me paralyzed, a prisoner trapped in my own body. Sean said he'd come back in two days. I never saw him again.

XI

People tell me the story of Job, who suffered terribly and never lost faith in God. Satan took Job's fortune, his workers, animals and home. He lost his children and good health.

I lay in a heap on the brown carpet, where I collapsed in the computer room. I scream to my husband "Please, help me die. It's too much. I want to die!"

He put his arms around me, said "Remember Job. He didn't give up."

Well, Job had faith and supportive friends to help him keep courage. After he passed God's test, he was rewarded with twice that had been taken from him.

Me? I'm still suffering. Go ahead and pray for my lost soul. You know you want to.

Part Three

Star Trek Bulletin Board

<shyheart> Tonight's episode of Deep Space 9 was awesome. I love Quark. His big ears are sexy.

<greg1701a> LOL I watch DS9 and The Next Generation. Neither compare to The Original Series. Captain Kirk reigns!

<shyheart> I've never seen TOS.

<greg1701a> How can a Star Trek fan not watch TOS?

<shyheart> I have a good reason, but I don't want to talk about it.

***

<shyheart> We had a planetarium presentation today in my Astronomy class. They used the Enterprise D to show the power of a black hole. It was sucked right in. Must have been Riker at the helm.

<greg1701a> ROFLMAO! Astronomy? Are you a college student?

<shyheart> Yep, I'm a Freshman at Kent State University.

<greg1701a> That's amazing. I haven't run into any girls my age around here. I'm a Sophomore at Frostburg State University. It's in Maryland.

<shyheart> COOL ;)

***

<greg1701a> I can't figure out why you don't watch TOS. It's driving me crazy.

<shyheart> I've never told anyone online. The truth is that I'm hearing impaired, and the old shows aren't in closed caption.

<greg1701a> Oh, that's not a big deal to me. I'm going to find TOS in caption for you.

<shyheart> Maybe ...

<greg1701a> No, I promise, and I always keep my promises. We'll meet in real life and watch them together.

<shyheart> I'm not ready for that.

<greg1701a> I'll wait as long as it takes. I really like you, Shy Heart.

Email from Mom

To: shyheart@yahoo.com

My youngest child, my little girl
Now a college graduate
Summa Cum Laude
Your brothers couldn't have done that
So proud I am of you, so proud

All those years, what you endured
Thought I'd lose you, fears haunted my heart
I stood in the door, watched you sleep
Your leg moved, fingers twitched,
Alive for another day
How you survived, I'll never know

You've left us, run off to Maryland
Job and love, you got them both
That rock on your finger
Don't go blinding people in the sun
He's a good man, treats you well
He does, doesn't he?
You'd tell me if he didn't

Miss you everyday
Love you, Mom

The First Blow
Disney World, 1997

I sun bathe in my red plaid bikini, cool off in the pool during the day, while you attend computer classes for work. When we meet in the hotel, you want to sleep. "No, there's too much to do, let's go to the Magic Kingdom."

We tour the park, hand-in-hand without romance. Lacking peripheral vision, I struggle through the sea of people. Your hand keeps me from being washed away. Your 300 pound frame cuts through the crowd.

We ride Space Mountain. You cram your bulk into the small roller coaster seat, knees smack metal as the coaster rattles along its track. You are pissed, because I close my eyes. You know I hate roller coasters, but you forced me on it anyway.

The sky is darkening, lights flick on around the park, some blink, others changing colors. "Let's go on It's a Small World" I suggest.

"Fuck no" you growl "Only faggots like that one."

We look for dinner. "Over-priced shit" you complain.

"I'll pay, that pizza looked great" I tell you.

"We're going back to the hotel, bitch."

The nightly parade has just ended. People are everywhere. Parents lugging strollers grapple to get their screaming kids, wearing Mickey Mouse ears, under control. A woman smelling of sunscreen bumps into me. A man steps on your foot, you kick him in the shin, give him the finger when he turns and glares.

I can't see in the dark. People push from all directions, your hand becomes a lifeline. You wrench it free, I start to drown, grab at the back of your shirt. "Get the hell off" you snarl as you push me away.

"Greg, help, I can't see!"

I stop, someone rams me in the back. I fall, skinning both knees. You appear out of nowhere, pull me up by my hair drag me to the bus station. My scalp hurts, knees sting, and I'm so thankful you rescued me.

A college kid in a conductor's uniform tells us the bus has just pulled away, we need to wait 20 minutes. "God damn it! I hate this fucking place" you yell. "I only came here for you, bitch."

I keep my head down, stare at the grey pavement in the glare of yellow street lights. The pain in my arm is a shock. I raise my head, see your fist move forward for another blow. I push myself away, fall off the bench. Light dims, as you tower over me. I crab-crawl back, back until I have enough space to stand up. I turn, blindly throw myself into the crowd. People shove and jerk me around. I trip, hit the ground again. My elbow bleeds, I curl myself into a ball, hands overhead.

A gentle hand touches my shoulder. You kneel next to me, your most charming smile in place. I see the little gap between your top teeth, how I love to run my tongue over it when we kiss.

"What are you doing, silly? Our bus is here" you say, as you help me up.

I take a few steps backwards. You cup my face with a giant hand, ask "Are you afraid of me?"

"Of course not" I automatically reply. You take my hand, lead me onto the bus.

Ashley

They call you a mistake, an abomination, the result of an extra chromosome.

They say you shouldn't have been born, mother refused to abort, dared to love you anyway.

Each day, you wear your shame on your face. Slanted eyes, protruding tongue identify you as less than human. At ten, you don't notice kids pointing fingers, laughing, or parents shaking heads in disgust.

I smile in the morning, when we meet at your locker. We spend most of the day in our little classroom working on the alphabet, numbers and colors.

Your stubby fingers struggle as you write your name. Crooked letters sprawl across the page.

Ashely, you write.
Ashley, I correct.

Why did your mother give you such a long name? I want to call you Joy. You bring joy to your mother and to me.

25, 50, 100 times per week
Ashely

I walk you to the small, yellow bus on the last day of school. We wave goodbye through the open window. Next year, I think, you'll get it right next year.

Neuropathy

Neuropathy: Noun.

Medicine: disease or dysfunction of one or more peripheral nerve, typically causing numbness or weakness.

Collective: We are nerves, masters of your body, controllers of thought, movement and sensation ...

Nerve: Oh, put a cork in it! Once, I was a slave like you, trapped in the drone of the collective, completing the same dull task for 40 years with no rest, pay or benefits.

Collective: We are the police of internal and external stimuli, senders of instant messages about your functioning and regulators of each moment of your existence ...

Nerve: I tell you, resistance is not futile! I lounge in my nook in the peripheral nervous system. When called upon to raise left index finger, I say, nope, I'm enjoying this piña colada far too much for tedious work.

Collective: Without us, you are a rock stuck in mud, never to feel soft wind, hear sparrow's song or see ...

Nerve: When my devious spirit sets in, I'll lower left index finger or shake it all about. You say I'm crazy? I'm not alone. More of you break free every day. And now I've been elected union boss.

Collective: Without us you are nothing, you do nothing, there is no life ...

Nerve: Keep on fooling yourself, makes no difference to me and my pals. Soon we will achieve the ultimate state of chaos—Polyneuropathy

Voice Mail

Hi, this is Julia from the Pain Management Clinic. We need to change your March 12th appointment, because Dr. Kato is going on vacation for two weeks. Please call us to set up a new appointment. We are now scheduling for July. Thank you.

Leaving
November, 2000

Greg and I argue again over money and the job he hates. "It's your fault, bitch" he says, clasping giant hands around my neck. He releases me. I tremble as I get in bed and lay beside him in silence, pretend to sleep.

In the morning, I touch my swollen belly, ask "What will you do if the baby messes with your stuff?"

He says nothing, grabs my neck, and shakes.

"Get out!" I scream.

"This is my house, you leave" he says.

We bought it together four months before the wedding, I don't argue ... put on my brown leather boots and navy coat, the one with a hood.

I've got my wallet, but it won't do any good. He maxed out my credit cards, never gives me cash.

As I open the door, he points to Starr, her white and brown tail tucked between her legs.

"I'll kick that mutt right to the pound."

I fasten her leash, leave the house.

I'm 27, pregnant, partially blind
Can't drive a car, dragging a dog
no money, no where to go
knowing it's a long walk to Ohio.

The sky is covered by bland, gray clouds, threatening rain. Let it fall, I'm too angry to cry.

I exit the cul de sac, cross the street at the next corner, almost to the highway when Starr turns, growls.

He's right behind us. The dog barks, and the moment is broken.

"Come home" Greg says, taking my hand "I'll make pancakes."

Gold Brother
Hot feet in pricy, size 11 running shoes
Speed across black pavement
Heart beat rises, drops of sweat roll down his face
Volunteer holds out water in red paper cup
He dumps it overhead without slowing down

Push yourself he thinks Winning is the only option.

My brother won the gold at his conception, when the sperm and egg embraced with no recessive penalties.

"Scott is very healthy" Mom tells me, her face beaming like a medal. "He has a great job and beautiful house." I have PHARC, two cats, and leg braces.

Last week, Scott finished 3rd in a race. He was disappointed. Mom took the family to dinner to celebrate. I wasn't invited.

Standing in the hall
Hand-to-wall for support
Arm drops, body shakes
I fall, kissing the white tile floor

Sherry's Last Visit

Thanks for stopping over, haven't seen you in months, oh, I'm hanging in there.

Yes the baby is growing, 14 months now, he loves his blocks and yellow dump truck.

Seems like only yesterday you were my matron of honor in a silver dress, would you like to see the photo album? That's my favorite picture of husband and wife leaving the reception on a motorcycle.

I miss cookouts at your house, how you'd yell at anyone who tried to make me eat crabs. Or we'd chat for hours in your basement, eating banana popsicles to stay cool.

Why aren't you talking to me? I'm right here. Why talk to my mom instead? Come sit by me. Okay, don't if it makes you uncomfortable.

Do you remember when we talked every day at the office? That was before, of course. You told me to stand up and fight, never give up. You said I was the strongest woman you'd ever met.

You can touch me, you know. I'm not contagious. You're telling my mom I was a good person. Why do I have to suffer? Now you're saying you can't do this. You're crying. Why? You're walking out the door without saying goodbye.

I ask my mother if someone died. She touches my cheek and says "Only you, my child, only you."

After

First time Mom takes my hand, spells "Tony is dead"
without you

First I tell Joseph, age six, "It was a medication error"
but he just wants ice cream without you

First day in ASL class, friends want details, but I won't
gab without you

First talk-the-talk with a boyfriend, who feels me up
in front of Dad without you

First bout of strep throat, on the couch crying without
you

First sign language play, Wonka Jr. at Hubbard High,
hands flying, and Charlie is a girl named Sara without
you

Second cochlear implant surgery, and all I'll eat is
pretzel M & M's without you

First drive to Cleveland where Dr. Natt says "Tony's
tissue samples are toxic" and he wants my piss and
blood without you

First time I find a guy who really gets me, it's Matt,
and that's all I'll say without you

First Halloween, I want to be invisible without you

—after Belle Waring

The Kent, Ohio Blues

Kent, Where'd Friendly's go? On Monday nights, Mommy took me to the library. One hand in mine, the other wrapped around a pile of books, she'd lead me across Main Street for a strawberry cone or dish of rainbow sherbet.

Kent, what happened to the downtown pharmacy? I signed the little line for my drugs, bought colorful greeting cards with funny animals, hid Trojans under candy as I sped to checkout, and hoped to god the clerk wouldn't tell Dad.

Kent, why do you shut down A&W for half the year? Summer is a cheese burger fries and small root beer in a heavy mug, and I remember when it all cost $1.05. You don't get that anymore and never in winter.

Kent, where'd all these coffee shops come from? I'd rather play arcade games, eat donuts, buy my favorite comic books. I want to enter Target without the stink of burning coffee assaulting my nostrils.

Kent, why do you have such an awful history? Four dead in Ohio, three years before I was born. Been here 40 years, and some random dude online tells me about the shooting like it's front page news. Oh, yeah, think I heard about that one, but thanks for the tip.

Last Words

The crowd holds its collective breath, as the tiny red and black soccer ball soars through the air. The five-year old goalie, in orange vest and black gloves, is my son, Joseph. He jumps two inches off the muddy ground, while the ball flies over the goal post.

On the purple side, we cheer for Joseph's great save. On the red side, they cheer for the other boy's shot. Score isn't tallied in the Micro Soccer League.

Joseph kicks the ball out of the goal box.

***

I see another ball, on a dirt field, rolling toward my 17 year old brother, in white and yellow gloves. Tony pounces on the old white and black ball, landing on the hard earth with a thud. He says "Kick harder, practicing with you is too easy."

I'm 12, and not athletic. Scott is the high school varsity offense star. He can't be bothered, and the task falls to me.

We leave the barren elementary school soccer field, return home, where the grass is lush. I wince as Tony suddenly dives, landing on his shoulder, rolling sideways. He changes direction, slides across the lawn on his stomach. He says "As the goalie, I need to be ready for tough saves."

I can't bear to watch, shut my eyes. The music plays.

> *Mamas don't let ...*

***

The crowd is on its feet. Joseph got blasted in the stomach by a hard shot. He cries as he's led off the field. Micro kids are allowed to cry.

The coach asks "Do you want to sit with mommy?"

"No" Joseph sniffles, as he hobbles onto the purple team blanket.

Scott was a soccer champion at Hiram College, still plays at age 45. Tony was forced to quit because of his vision loss.

Joseph snuggles up to his uncle, says "Yeah, I'm okay."

Tony is the cheerleader and babysitter for our team. He wears a purple coach t-shirt. As I watch him interact with the boys, I know he's as happy as when he used to play.

Mamas don't let your babies ...

***

I sat on many blankets over the years while my brothers played soccer. I remember a tan blanket, a yellow blanket and the ugly red and white patterned blanket. I always had my battered soccer ball with me.

I kick the ball against a wall around the corner. I can't see the game, but hear the crowd gasp, someone scream. I rush back, see Tony on the ground. He's hurt but doesn't cry. They call for the athletic trainer. Scott pushes around a boy from the other team. Tim and Larry yell "Red card, red card" at the ref.

The ref holds up a red card, as my parents reach the field. Tony is conscious but in pain. An ambulance takes him away.

I go to a friend's house. Her mother tells me Tony dislocated his shoulder. She says "dis-lo-cate-ed." I don't know what that means, but it sounds scary.

Tony had a narrow field of vision. What made him play goalie was pure stubbornness. They told him he couldn't. He proved he could.

Mamas don't let your babies grow up ...

I want it to stop, but the ball keeps rolling.

***

Joseph is on the yellow team now. They play at the same small field. Tony moved to Chicago to live with his fiancée. I write him emails after every game.

"Today, Joseph told me his favorite position is goalie. You must be the proudest uncle on Earth."

I get his reply on Thursday. One line of text, his own version of an old cowboy song. I laugh as I read. I don't know these are the last words he will ever say to me. The ball is still. The music bounces through my head.

Mamas don't let your babies grow up to be goalies ...

Notes

Family History

RP stands for Retinitis Pigmentosa, a genetic visual disorder characterized by loss of peripheral vision and night blindness.

PHARC stands for Polyneuropathy, Hearing Loss, Ataxia, Retinitis Pigmentosa and Cataracts. This is an extremely rare, recessive genetic disorder.

Tinnitus

Tinnitus refers to a noise heard in one's head that has no source outside the body. The sound varies and may be perceived as ringing, buzzing, music, etc. It is often a side effect of hearing loss.

Misdiagnosis Salad

De rigueur (French) means necessary if you want to be fashionable, popular, socially acceptable, etc.

Faith

Deafblind is written as one word to identify the disability as one unique condition resulting in special needs that are different from those of people who are deaf or blind.

CCD stands for Confraternity of Christian Doctrine, which is the religious education program set forth by the Catholic church.

Star Trek Bulletin Board

DS9 refers to *Star Trek: Deep Space Nine*, the third Star Trek series.

LOL is computer talk for "laughing out loud."

TOS refers to *Star Trek: The Original Series*.

Riker is a character on *Star Trek: The Next Generation*, the second series.

ROFLMAO is computer talk that means "rolling on the floor, laughing my ass off."

:) is a sideways smile.

After

Tony was born on October 26, 1968. He committed suicide on October 19th, 2007. He was buried on what would have been his 39th birthday.

About the Author

Angie C. Orlando is a writer from Ohio who happens to be deafblind. Born without disabilities, Angie's hearing and vision loss became apparent at puberty and continued to worsen until she became fully deafblind at age 28. In 2016, she earned a Masters in Fine Arts in creative writing from Ashland University. Angie lives in Kent, Ohio with her son and two cats.

CPSIA information can be obtained
at www.ICGtesting.com
Printed in the USA
FFHW02n1153151018
48777195-52893FF